The Beginner's Guide to Raising A Happy Guinea Pig

A Simple, Practical Guide to Guinea Pig Care

By
Amanda Hewitt

Table of Contents:

5

Introduction:
What's a Guinea Pig, Anyway?

Guinea pigs - small, cute, adorable, and at first glance, a wonderful family pet that takes little work and forethought. Like a goldfish, hermit crab, or some other small animal...right?

Wrong!

Guinea pigs, who are actually members of the rodent family, are native to South America. Ironically, they're not pigs, and they certainly aren't from Guinea.

Because of domestication, the guinea pig isn't actually found in the wild anymore. It's almost impossible to imagine these small, fuzzy creatures crawling over fallen logs and sleeping under the open skies.

Some people even competitively show and breed the guinea pig, though many guinea pigs simply live the 'good life', resting at home in a comfortable cage, with family who loves them.

Are Guinea Pigs Intelligent?

The big assumption that many parents have when they purchase a guinea pig for their children is that guinea pigs are stupid. This assumption is simply wrong! When you take into account their size, they're extremely intelligent animals, and owners often admit to being 'hassled' by their guinea pigs for love, attention, and treats.

Famous for their 'Wheek!', a squeak of sorts, this noise isn't made in the wild. It's often reserved for their owners, and the promise of a treat coming from the fridge.

Who Are Guinea Pigs Good For?

A guinea pig *is not* a pet that you can purchase and then casually 'forget about', and actually are a wonderful animal that deserves a good home with someone who will care from them.

Guinea pigs are often thought of as a child's pet, however, they're good pets for anyone who is looking for an affectionate animal that enjoys being both held and played with.

Guinea pigs are actually a wonderful pet for someone who needs a pet to love and nurture, for all ages. And if you're looking for a pet in a small apartment, a guinea pig is perfect!

Want to Learn More?

Ready to take a journey of not only learning, but discovery? The guinea pig is a great pet, a wonderful companion, and is an absolutely incredible animal. All you have to do is discover why.

Chapter One:
The History of the Guinea Pig

The Guinea Pig
Scientific Name: Cavia Porchellus
Also Known As: Cavie, Cavy, Cy
History: Detailed!
Use: An endearing pet, and wonderful companion. Also sometimes used for dinner.

The guinea pig has a long, colorful, and *unique* history to call their own. When you're taking care of this little critter, you're not just taking care of a pet. You're really taking care of a wild and proud animal.

While guinea pigs are originally found in the wild of North America, they've been highly domesticated - to the point that you simply can't find them there, in fact.

The guinea pig was brought over by European traders in the 16th century, and since then have enjoyed life has a house pet - mostly because of their docile, passive nature and loving attitude.

In North America guinea pigs are a large part of the culture and were often hunted for food purposes. They're also used in religious ceremonies and even folk medicine.

Reports suggest that the guinea pig was domesticated as early as 5000 BC as a source of food, and statues of the guinea pig were unearthed in both Peru and Ecuador dating from 500 BC to 500 AD.

Surprisingly, the Moche people of Peru often worshiped animals, and the guinea pig is commonly seen in their art. Between 1200 AD to roughly 1532 (The Spanish Conquest), guinea pigs were selectively bred into numerous varieties. Looking at modern breeds, you can sometimes see the roots of this.
Folklore surrounding the guinea pig is wide, and it's not uncommon to find them as a part of daily social and religious encounters - including guinea pigs being exchanged as gifts.

Even today, the guinea pig plays a large role in the medicines of many people and villages. In areas in the Andes, where Western medicine is either distrusted or simply unavailable, the guinea pig is used to help cure a whole number of illnesses, including arthritis and jaundice.

So, Why Pigs?

Every wonder why the guinea pig is indeed called a guinea *pig*, especially considered that it has little related to a pig! So, why are they commonly called *pigs*?

Well, that's not really known! It's thought that they may have been called pigs because of the sounds they emit. One of their distinctive squeals sounds very similar to the sound a pig makes.

However, they are somewhat built like a small pig - a large head in comparison to their body, a stout neck and a rounded back end with no real tail.

Guinea pigs are also known for spending a lot of time eating, which is associated as a pig quality.

Yet another possible reason for the name is that they tend to spend a lot of time in a confined area, mostly their cage. Very similar to a 'pig pen', and for this reason they were easily transported on ships.

Also, the 'porcellus' in the scientific name, cavia porcellus, means 'little pig'. So many different pig references for an animal that has no relationship with one!

When... Giant Guinea Pigs Ruled The Earth?!

Ever heard of the town of Urumaco? Yeah, neither had we. But it's in Venezuela, about 250 miles west of Caracas. What's in this town of Urumaco?

The remains of what can only be described as a giant rodent. Fossils in the surrounding areas suggest that this area was lush with a beautiful, tropical landscape.

Roaming this gorgeous paradise were giant animals - no joke! Along some of the other finds in this area stuffed with well preserved fossils are 10 foot long turtles, catfish that would win any tournament around now, 10 foot tall flightless, carnivorous birds, marsupial cats the size of lions, and even 33 foot long crocodiles!

The rodent that they found were the first of their kind to be found, and is clearly the relative to the wonderful little pets we keep today. These creatures probably enjoyed the sea grass near an ancient river, and lived roughly 8 million years ago.

The rodent's scientific name is Phoberomys pattersoni (Named after the paleontologist who did work in the field), this 'little' guy was 9 feet long, stood a proud 4 feet tall, and weighed more than **1,500 pounds**. Try keeping *that* in a cage! What's more, the incredibly complete skeleton of this unusual rodent had about 8 inches worth of front teeth.

They suspect that Phoberomys was semi-aquatic, and actually formed herds. Just picture this - numerous giant guinea pig with a long tail to balance themselves running through a tropical paradise. Amazing.

The History of Experiments

If you look up the term ' guinea pig' in the dictionary, you're not just going to get the cute a fuzzy mammal. Chances are, the term 'something to be experimented on' is going to be run across.

Guinea pigs have a surprisingly long and detailed history of being used in experiments for science, mostly because we share a certain evolutionary quirk - neither of us can manufacture vitamin C.

No other creature has to get their vitamin C from food like the two of us, so that's created a unique bond. In fact, the reason that vitamin C was discovered is because of research done on a guinea pig.

But don't scream at science just yet - because of the experiments that were conducted on guinea pigs, we have medicines for a whole mess of things, including asthma, tuberculosis, diphtheria, and more.

Even the replacement heart valve, something that's saved countless lives, can be attributed to the guinea pig. And while they're not the experimental animal of choices (Because of low birth rates and surprisingly long gestation), they are sometimes still used in different experiments.

Chapter Two:
Guinea Pig Variety

Do I Want a Long Haired Guinea Pig, or a Short Haired Guinea Pig?

Ah, a question for the ages. Guinea pig breeds are primarily distinguished by their hair, so when you go to choose a breed, you have to decide if you want a long haired guinea pig or a short haired guinea pig.

Short haired guinea pigs are, without a doubt, easier to take care of then a long haired guinea pig. They require little brushing to be groomed and don't have too many issues related to their hair.

A long haired guinea pig is going to take a great deal more work, so you should never purchase one without being positive you can groom them properly.

You need to brush a long haired guinea pig daily to ensure that their hair doesn't tangle, and some even go as far as to put pet-safe produces to help avoid tangling and promote shine.

Remember that short haired guinea pigs are just as beautiful as their long haired counterpart, and personality-wise, they will both love you the same. Don't choose just by the hair - the guinea pig is really who you need to take care of.

While we've listed the breeds, you need to realize that personality wise, there is little difference between these guinea pigs. The difference lies solely in looks, so if you just want a good personality, go with a less exotic guinea pig!

Note:

Unless noted, these breeds are easy to groom. There are very few breeds of Guinea pigs that are actually difficult to groom, but know that the longer their hair is, the more difficulty you're going to experience with them.

Long haired guinea pigs aren't recommended for family, but for show - unless you choose to keep the hair trimmed.

The Abyssinian

One of the oldest breeds of guinea pigs, the Abyssinian is a unique pig that is most often used as a show guinea pig. The distinctive rosettes (swirls in the hair) make this guinea pig stand out from the rest.

To be shown, the Abyssinian needs to have at least eight separate rosettes, but most prefer ten. He tends to be a conversational topic for those who have never seen one before, and make a wonderful pet.

The lifespan of the Abyssinian is about eight years, but can live longer if he's from a healthy background and has been taken care of properly. He's also an extremely cuddly pet that will have no trouble crawling up in your lap and lying with you.

This guinea pig needs to be well groomed, but the fur tends to be difficult to take care of, because it grows in many different ways. If you're looking for a low maintenance pet, this certainly isn't one!

The American Guinea Pig

This is another of the oldest breeds recorded - the American guinea pig is the 'classic' guinea pig, so to speak, and most commonly found. Don't take this for boring, though, because these little critters have a wonderful personality and are extremely loving.

If you're looking for a pet that's suitable for a young child, this is certainly it. Because of their short, smooth fur, this guinea pig is easy to groom and takes very little time to care for.

However, if you're looking for a show guinea pig, try something more exotic. While the American guinea pig comes in a variety of different colors, it's not what you would call the most 'exciting' piggy in the pen.

Peruvian

Oh my! The ultimate indulgence in long haired guinea pigs, the Peruvian's hair can grow over a foot in length, and is most known for the soft, gentle 'sweeps' of hair that enfold the entire body.

This is mostly a show guinea pig, and many people simply don't recommend a Peruvian as a family pet because of the tremendous amount of work that goes into taking care of them.

A unique and interesting thing about the Peruvian is that their hair actually grows out from their head, covering it entirely. When viewed from the top, they look like little round puddles of hair!

Satin: This breed has a 'satin' counterpart, which means that they have the same characteristics, but the coat feels like satin to the touch, with a glossy coat over it.

Silkie

Also called a 'sheltie', the silkie is an adorable loving pet that has many wonderful qualities. They're extremely similar to the Peruvian, but they don't have a long sweep of hair that covers their head. Instead, their hair sweeps back, forming a mane of sorts.

From above, this adorable pet greatly resembles a teardrop. Their hair is both softer and shinier than the Peruvian, but is still extremely difficult to care for.

Satin: This breed has a 'satin' counterpart, which means that they have the same characteristics, but the coat feels like satin to the touch, with a glossy coat over it.

Teddy

The teddy guinea pig has a short, dense coat that tends to be very wiry. The hair of the Teddy is kinked, and resilient. Their body is most like the American guinea pig, and sometimes resembles a stuffed animal.

They have a wonderful personality, and their nose has a unique upturn called a 'Roman nose' that looks not only interesting, but gives their face an 'inquisitive' look to it.

Satin*:* This breed has a 'satin' counterpart, which means that they have the same characteristics, but the coat feels like satin to the touch, with a glossy coat over it.

White Crested

The white crested is easy to spot, as they're clearly defined by their white, circular rosette on the very top of their forehead. This certainly makes the guinea pig stand out of the crowd!

A true white crested guinea pig will have no other white on his body, but come in all sorts of different colors. A white crested guinea pig with white anywhere else cannot be showed.

Texel

You can't imagine the looks that this guinea pig gets when people simply don't expect it! The texel guinea pig has long, soft hair that forms curls over the entire body (even the belly).

The hair is very thick, almost to make up for their small, compact body and broad head. This is one of the most difficult breeds to keep groomed, because their hair is so prone to tangling!

Other Color Selections:

In addition to the normal breeds, there are color varieties that are sometimes confused with breeds. These are absolutely adorable, and really are quite unique!

Self: A self guinea pig refers to a solid colored guinea pig, which includes black, white, beige, red, chocolate, lilac, cream, and blue.

Brindle: The brindle is a mingling of two colors, one dark and one light, appearing all over the body of the guinea pig.

Dutch: The Dutch coloring is a guinea pig with a colored head that has a white blaze, with the front half and the back half having the same color.

Tortoiseshell: This guinea pig has clearly defined rectangular patches of black and red distributed uniformly across the entire body. These patches do not run together.

Tortoiseshell and White: With this guinea pig, clearly defined rectangular patches of white, red, and black are around the pig with the dividing line running down the middle of the back and the belly. The colors should be switched when looking at the line.

Roan: Dark black or red hairs are mixed together evenly on the guinea pig.

Albino: The albino is a classic - a guinea pig that is completely white, with pink eyes instead of black eyes.

Dalmatian: A dalmatian guinea pig is a white guinea pig with dark spots over the entire body, very similar to the dog breed.

Agouti: Alternating bands of dark and light over the entire body, most commonly silver and gold colors.

Himalayan: A Himalayan guinea pig has an all white body, with a dark nose, ears, and feet. They often have red eyes.

Chapter Three:
Choosing a Guinea Pig

So, you know what guinea pig breed you want - or you at least have an idea of how much time you can spend with your guinea, and you're able to choose what you can't take care of - right?

Well, if you don't, go back and read Chapter Two, which outlines the different breeds and what makes them special - basically, what sets them apart from each other.

In this chapter, we're going to talk about how you can choose *your* guinea pig from the rest of the pack. Not just about how you can tell a healthy guinea from a sick guinea, but how you can just know that this little one is what you need.

Don't be afraid to print out this entire chapter and take it with you when you go to purchase your guinea pig, as it's important that you know who you want to spend the rest of his life with.

One Guinea Pig, Two Guinea Pig, Three Guinea Pig, *More*

Many families opt for one guinea pig because it would be cheaper and easier to care for, and some people have six or more guinea pigs in their home at one time, with several cages to avoid fighting.

While one guinea pig is probably enough to keep you entertained and alert, you should put some serious thought into purchasing two guinea pigs or more.

Not only are guinea pigs extremely social creatures, they love the company of others. They can get lonely by themselves, and their health will suffer if left alone.

"Well, two guinea pigs are more work!" Many parents cry when their children ask for not one but two of the adorable rodents. However, that entire mindset is completely wrong.

Guinea pigs need attention, and if you have just one, your Guinea pig is going to get lonely very fast and cry for your attention more often. If he or she has a partner or playmate to keep them entertained, you don't have to spend quite as much time with them.

And considering that guinea pigs are extremely inexpensive pets to begin with, it's not going to strain your budget.

The Sex of the Matter

If you're going to just get a guinea pig, sex doesn't matter too much. By nature, female guinea pigs are going to be more docile and less active, while their male counterparts are going to have more energy and need more exercise.

A common misconception with male guinea pigs is that if you put two in the same cage, they're going to fight to the death. That is nothing but wrong.

Two male guinea pigs *will* fight if they don't have enough cage space, but given plenty room, each guinea pig will have his own territory and be content with it.

If you have two male guinea pigs, you *cannot* introduce a female guinea pig to the cage. The males will fight for dominance (and the female), and the loser would have to be removed from the cage immediately.

If he's left there, he will starve to death as the dominate male will keep him away from both the food and water.

Two females in the same cage will get along well, but you may find that they will 'bicker' a bit over food and water. Because of their docile nature, however, it's very unlikely that a major fight will break out.

A male and a female in the same cage will actually get along best. The female acknowledges that the male is dominant, and the male accepts the female as his, and act peacefully towards her.

The only problem with this peaceful situation? The puppies (the term for baby guinea pigs) that can happen when you leave a male and a female unattended.

The female cycle is only 18 days, and the gestation of guinea pigs are only two months. While this is relatively long for rodents, it's very possible that two lively guinea pigs can give birth to literally dozens of puppies in just a year.

The best thing you can do in this situation is get one of the two guinea pigs neutered, because you'll eliminate the possible issues associated with having puppies running around!

I'm Staring at my Guinea Pigs... Help!

Many pet stores will have at least one cage of guinea pigs, if not two or more. It's simply that guinea pigs give birth *a lot*, and there is a demand for the puppies they produce.

If you're purchasing more then one, make sure to get two from the same cage. This will take care of any of the issues that might arise from fighting in their cage.

Where Should I Buy My Guinea Pig?

There are actually many options open to you if you're searching for somewhere to purchase a brand new guinea pig for a pet, or for showing. You probably didn't even know you *had* so many options available to you!

The pet store is actually the most common place that people go to buy a guinea pig, but you need to make sure that they're being treated properly there.

Look for clean bedding, and cages that separate the males and females when they get old enough. Otherwise you might bring home a guinea pig and discover that she was pregnant!

Your pet-store guinea pig also should have a good diet, so ask the staff exactly what they're feeding them and how they're being taken care of. Show your knowledge and see if they're doing what they need to be to keep the guinea pigs in good health.

One final thing to consider when you're buying from a pet store is socialization. If the staff aren't handling them, they're going to be extremely skittish. While it's normal that they won't appreciate strangers prodding them, some socialization is important.

If you're looking for a show guinea pig, you're most likely to find a good one with a guinea pig breeder. You can search online, or in your local paper, to see if there are any in your area.

A good breeder is going to ensure that your guinea pig is handled from a very young age, and that they're very social creatures. You can even discuss the exact diet that guinea pig is on, so that he'll feel right at home as soon as you put him in his new cage.

And finally, you have the option of getting a guinea pig from a shelter. Yes, there are actually guinea pig shelters out there, so do a search to find out where the closest one to you is.

You could also just check your phone book, and see if you can find one that's in the same zip code as you. This is sometimes easier then going online, but not always.

If you can't find a guinea pig shelter either way, your last resort should be to call the ASPCA and see if they have a listing of guinea pig shelters either in your area.

Getting your guinea pigs from a shelter is one of the greatest things that you can do for an animal, because you're really giving this little piggy a second chance at a wonderful home and family.

Most of the time, guinea pigs who end up in shelters aren't there because they're mean, nasty, or sick. Those that owned them before simply couldn't take care of them, had to move, or weren't good guinea pig parents.

It's likely that a guinea pig from a shelter is going to be a bit skittish, but many will settle right in with you as soon as they fall into a comfortable routine.

Where ever you get a guinea pig, make sure that he's in good health (see below!) and that he's going to be the piggy for you. Personality plays a big factor, so don't just consider looks.

Healthy Piggy

There are a number of ways to spot a guinea pig who simply isn't healthy, and you shouldn't bring an unhealthy pig into your home - especially if he's going to be introduced to another pig.

On the next page, we've put a check list to print out and take with you, so you can be sure the guinea pig who has captured your heart is healthy and ready to be loved.

The Health Chart

-   Your guinea pig should be alert and active unless he is sleeping. He should be aware that you're near and even playing with other guinea pigs in the cage.

-   The guinea pig's nose, eyes, and ears should be free of discharge, and clean.

-   The coat of the guinea pig should be full, thick, and soft. Pet him a few times to see if you can find any bald patches or irritated areas. A little ruffle from playing is normal.

-   The skin of the guinea pig should be checked for redness or flakes, which is a sure sign of an issue.

-   You should check the skin and fur for parasites such as lice which can harm the guinea pig.

–   The guinea pig should be plump, rounded, and firm. Guinea pigs should not be overly skinny or grossly overweight as this is a sign of healthy issues or possible health issues in the future.

A Guinea Pig is a Long Term Pet

Don't regard your guinea as a goldfish or short term pet experience. With a lifespan between 7 and 10 years, a guinea pig is *not* a pet that should be taken lightly.

Consider this: If you purchase two guinea pigs for your child when he's only 10 years old, he could still be caring for them when he gets his first girlfriend, gets his heart broken for the first time, goes to prom and yes, even graduates high school.

The Average Price of a Guinea Pig

So, not sure how much not just your guinea pig, but the supplies are going to set you back? Have no fear. We have the basic idea of not only what you're going to spend, but how much time you need to dedicate to this adorable little creature.

For a guinea pig that's not a show pig, you can expect to pay between $5 to $15 for each pig and up to $45 for a pedigree pig or a long haired guinea pig.

A good quality cage is going to cost you between $30-60, but making your own large cage can cost as little as $35, and you get much more room for your guinea pigs to roam.

You're going to need grooming tools (check out the grooming chapter for more information), but these won't set you back much at all - $15 at most for the majority of owners, and grooming only takes about 30 minutes a month for short haired, or 2-3 hours for long haired pigs.

You also want to remember that food isn't expensive with guinea pigs, but they do love to chew. Estimate the price of veggies and factor in pellets, which cost as little as $10 a bag.

Hay is very cheap when bought in bulk, and lasts long enough that your guinea pig will enjoy all of it. The bedding is only between $5-10 a bag, and you need to change it once a week.

Overall, the guinea pig is very low maintenance, as far as pets go, and you can really have a wonderful animal to love and care for, all for very little money and time.

Guinea Pigs as a Companion Animal

Guinea pigs aren't just for children - they make wonderful pets for those in their 20's and 30's looking for someone to come home to after work, and can be great companions for the elderly.

While no studies have been done on this subject, many people swear to the use of a guinea pig as a companion animal for the elderly who can get lonely, but don't have the energy to take care of a dog or cat.

Because of their docile nature and love of attention, they really make wonderful pets for *anyone* who wants someone to love and take care of. As long as you remember that a guinea pig isn't a toy, but a real, live animal, you can have a strong and powerful bond forming.

Chapter Four:
Housing your Guinea Pig

Sit down and pull out a piece of paper because when you go out and buy a guinea pig, you're going to need something to put the little bugger in. And more importantly, he's going to need to like this area!

Remember to take time in choosing his home, because while it's just a cage to you - something that sits in the corner, more a decoration then anything else - it's going to be your pets home and the area he spends the most time in.

There are also a lot of *other* things he's going to need, including food, toys, and yes, things to chew on. Because he's in the rodent family, his teeth never stop growing. To keep them clean, sharp, and healthy, he needs to chew... a *lot*.

But we're going to get to those things in a bit. The first aspect you need to pay attention to is your brand new pet's home.

The Cage

Walk into any pet store and you're going to find *many* cages. Different sizes, shapes, and types are going to greet you. Some might be specially for the guinea pig, while others are for small critters in general.

Your cage should be big enough that two or more guinea pigs can run free. I'm not saying you need a *giant* cage, but leaving your guinea pig in a tight space his entire life simply isn't fair.

Basically, the bigger, the better. Whatever your budget allows for, of course. But if you can afford a larger cage, your guinea pig is going to thank you with love and happiness. If you plan on having two or more (which is recommended), you should always choose a larger size.

Your cage of choice should not have a wire bottom, but instead a more solid bottom. A plastic bottom is the most common that you can find.

A slide-out area for easy cleaning is also a good choice, but not needed. So make sure that this is a second on your list of must-haves for a cage.

A big door is also a good addition to a guinea pig's cage. And make sure that you have plenty of room to get your hand in and pet, love, and pick up your piggy.

Note:

I'm sure you've read somewhere that 2.5 square feet per guinea pig is enough room, but anyone who has ever owned a guinea pig can tell you that it's simply not enough.

Estimate about 7.5 square feet for one, or 10.5 for two. Sound like a lot? Not when you consider overweight guinea pigs are more likely to have a considerable amount of health problems, and that the more exercise a guinea pig gets, the happier he's going to be.

If you simply can't find a big enough one, consider making your own guinea pig cage to house your new pet. It won't take you very long, and it's extremely rewarding - not only because you'll have a cage that your guinea pig really loves, but because it will without a doubt outshine anything you could have purchased.

Bedding

Ah, the root of the matter - bedding. A lot of people think that throwing a towel down is an 'okay' option, but it's simply *not*. There are specific beddings that can and can't be used for your pig.

Pine shavings are an absolute 'no', as they can literally poison your pets. Aspen shavings are an okay choice, but hay is something that's the best option - and it's also cheap.

Cedar shavings are also extremely dangerous for your guinea pig. They're known to cause respiratory problems, and sometimes your guinea pig can become allergic to them. The main reason that they're dangerous is because of the oils that are responsible for the distinctive scent. This scent often covers the urine scent, but no matter how tempting, this is a dangerous thing to give to your pet.

Aspen shavings are very safe for your guinea pig, but it can be extremely expensive, and has absolutely no odor control. You're going to smell what your pet does, no matter what.

Straw as a bedding should be avoided completely. It doesn't absorb droppings at all, does nothing for the scent, and what's worse, it's rough, which means it can cause injuries to your guinea pigs.

One of the more popular alternatives to the normal wood shavings is called CareFRESH. It's actually made from wood pulp fibers that can't be processed into paper, and they look sort of like shredded egg cartons.

The best thing about CareFRESH is the odor control, which inhibits the formation of the ammonia that gives guinea pig 'messes' their unpleasant smell.

Crown pellet bedding is something that many people prefer, which is made from recycled newspaper and compressed into pellets. It has wonderful odor control like CareFRESH, and works best when used under a softer bedding, like Timothy hay (see below). It's far too dense to be the sole bedding.

Some who are looking for an 'organic' option appreciate corn cob bedding, which can be soft and easy on your pet. However, be careful with it, because it can grow mold much faster then other bedding.

The best option, without a doubt, is Timothy hay. Not only does it provide a wonderful and delicious food source for your guinea pigs, but it's soft enough that they can actually play with it.

Really, they do! Guinea pigs love tunneling into the hay and making nests to sleep, so their bed is extra soft and incredibly comfortable. When fresh, it has a wonderful scent.

If you're going to go with Timothy hay (even coupled with a pellet bedding), it's best to buy it fresh directly from a gardening store or farm supply company. Many times, a farmer himself will sell it to you if you explain why you need it.

Supplies

What else do you need to keep your little guinea pig happy and content? Well, not too much. For the most part, guinea pigs are easy to please and content with what they have.

You're going to absolutely need somewhere for your guinea pig to 'hide'. Because they're animals of prey in the wild, when scared or tired they often choose to hide somewhere out of sight.

There are a lot of choices for you in this regard, and the more places your guinea pig has, the better.

A PVC pipe works not only as a hiding place, but it makes a great tunnel for your pet to play with and explore. This keeps him active and enjoying it.

An overturned container with a hole in it for climbing in and out works as well, so take your time in the pet store and see what they have.

For their water, the use of a drinking bottle is the best option. It's easy for them to use, and easy to fill up. Your guinea pig also can't knock it over or down when he gets bored.

A hay rack is a good choice for people who also use fresh hay as their bedding. This means that your guinea pig won't be eating soiled hay between changing's, and many pigs love to pull long strands out of the rack for fun.

Many people love to 'change it up' with their terrain, and add rocks, bricks, and tubes for playing in. We've already covered putting in PVC pipe for a lot of fun. Don't forget that elbow and 'T' joints are a wonderful addition!

Bricks are very cheap additions, and rocks are often free. This will ensure that your guinea pig's claws aren't getting out of hand, and they love to climb and get exercise. This also keeps them agile and active.

Don't forget balls! Something that moves is a big hit with guinea pigs, and they provide nearly endless hours of enjoyment. Mirrors are also fun for guinea pigs.

As far as food is concerned, the use of a clay bowl is a good option, because it can't be knocked into anything. A bored guinea pig can often get into trouble if you let them!

Basic Guinea Hygiene

Keeping up the health of your guinea pig includes cleaning out the cage, but what exactly do you have to do to ensure that your guinea pigs hygiene is top notch?

Each day you should remove uneaten food, and take out urine areas or dropping. Soiled bedding can be gently removed from the guinea pig house without much problem at all.

Once a week, you need to completely remove the bedding and scrub the entire cage with hot, soapy water. Make sure that it's rinsed thoroughly afterwards to avoid soapy residue. They dry before you add fresh bedding and food.

Your Guinea Pig First Aid Kit

Guinea pigs are active, and that goes to say that they can sometimes get into trouble. You don't have to go to the vet for every nick, scrape, cut and bruise your guinea pig gets - you can do a lot at your home.

Below is a checklist of things that you should buy as a base for your guinea pig first aid kit, and why. We put it in a separate page so that you can easily print just that page, and take it to the pet store.

Note:

If you can only have one thing on the entire list, make it the hydrogen peroxide solution. You can clean wounds, and ears, as well as induce vomiting if your guinea pig has eaten something that could poison him.

Guinea Pig First Aid Kit Checklist

3% hydrogen peroxide solution
Antibiotic ointment for small cuts and scrapes
Artificial tear gel
Anti-itch spray (available at all pet stores) for itching, dermatitis, or abrasions
Ear wipes
Eye wipes
Bitter apple spray, to keep your guinea pig from licking their wounds
Bandages, small and large. Keep a wide assortment of gauze and stretch bandages for all sorts of issues
First aid lotion
Mild dishwashing detergent that cuts grease for cleaning wounds.
Cotton balls and swabs

Other Things you Might Want:

Saline solution to flush the eyes
Syringe (no needle)
Latex gloves
Tweezers
Tick release ointment
Rectal thermometer
Vaseline
Penlight

A storage container to keep
everything organized and clean.

You're going to want to keep your first aid
kit in a cool, dry area - perhaps the back of
a closet or hidden in a drawer. You **do not**
want to keep it in the bathroom because of
the moisture that's made from a shower or
bath.

Not Sure What's Normal?

Take your little piggy's temperature, but not
sure if this is normal or not? Don't feel bad
- it's much different from ours, so use this
chart as an indication on what's right and
what's wrong.

Normals For a Guinea Pig

Temperature: 100 - 102.5 F
Pulse: 250-300 beats per minute
Respiration: 80-90 respirations per minute

Chapter Five:
Feeding Your Guinea Pig

So you need to know what's safe for your guinea pig to eat. If you don't think you need to know, you're wrong - because guinea pigs can't eat just anything.

They have a diet, and they like it. Knowing what is and is not safe for your guinea pig to consume is important, because you don't want to accidentally poison your pet with a normal, household item that you thought he would enjoy.

For the most part, guinea pigs have a wide variety of foods they eat. Just remember that they certainly don't eat meat, and you already have a good start!

The Schedule

You'll see this several times during this book, but the fact remains the same. guinea pigs are comforted by a normal schedule, and can get very stressed if something changes. That means that you should strive to clean their cage and feed them at the same time.

Guinea pigs can also become upset if you abruptly change their food, so try and stick with the same thing if at all possible. Treats are one thing, but their main food source is a completely different thing.

To Each His Own

Every guinea pig is different in their favorite choices, and some guinea pigs have very discriminating tastes. Some prefer one thing, while others love another.

Test things with your guinea pigs, and slowly introduce it into their diet. Remember that eating too many fruits and vegetables at one time will cause diarrhea, so while it's tempting to lavish them with foods they love, make sure to ration properly.

What Guinea Pigs Can't Eat

There are very specific things that your guinea pig *can't* eat, so keep these in mind as you're searching for the Next Great Treat for your loveable guinea pig.

-Meat
-Dairy products
-Corn
-Tomato leaves
-Anything that has sugar in it
-Potatoes
-Raw beans
-Rhubarb
-Iceberg lettuce

Many owners like to experiment with guinea pig 'treat sticks' that are commercially available. Made from nuts and seeds with honey holding it all together, they look like a good option, but these often have sunflower seeds in their shell, which are a big choking hazard.

What Guinea Pigs Can Eat - and Love

We're going to list what your guinea pig will most likely love to eat, and we've put it on a separate page so that you can print it out, if you so desire, and bring it with you to the grocery store.

Even if you don't want to print your list out, it's easy to jump to it and find exactly what you need. Don't be afraid to experiment with these things, as you'll soon find the treat that your pet is going to really love.

What Your Guinea Pig Can Eat

-Apples

-Carrots and baby carrots

-Loose leaf lettuce

-Tomatoes

-Spinach

-Kale

-Small cubes of celery

-Crunchy, slightly stale bread (no mold!)

-Kiwi

-Green, red, and yellow peppers

-Parsley

-Florida oranges

-Mustard greens

-Dandelion greens

-Broccoli flower clusters

-Timothy hay

-Commercially available 'Berry crunchies'

Your pet's main diet should be made up of mostly Timothy hay and commercially available food pellets, complimented by the fresh fruits and vegetables that you can purchase.

You should strive for a pellet that has 20% crude protein and 16% fiber, and make sure that it has some vitamin C listed in the label, as guinea pigs are unable to produce it themselves.

Some of the best foods for them are simple grass (untreated by chemicals, of course), carrots, and tomatoes because of the high levels of vitamin C that are found.

What To Absolutely Avoid

What should you steer away from completely, or risk poisoning and even killing your innocent little guinea pig? A lot, but we're going to cover the basics.

For one, you should avoid potato peels. Some books say they're fine in small amounts, while others claim they're poisonous. Simply avoiding them altogether is a very easy way to avoid the confusion that arises.

Mixed treats that have nuts, seeds, or any dye at all should be avoided completely, because it really give your little guinea pig bad stomach problems.

Dried fruit often has sugar added, and it's simply not good for digestion. Give them fresh fruit if they really want something sweet.

Mineral wheels have been known to cause bladder stones, which can make urinating extremely painful for a guinea pig. While not definitive, you should still avoid them.

Multivitamins aren't healthy for your guinea pig, as excess vitamins A and D can cause serious health problems. Giving small doses of plain vitamin C is safe, however.

Long celery stalks are something that should be avoided at all cost, because the long strands are nearly impossible for the guinea pig to digest properly. This means that they can get severely sick eating them.

And finally, most commercial pet treats for guinea pigs should be highly avoided. The empty calories in the fat and sugars will end up depriving your pet of the essential foods that he really needs to stay healthy and feel good. Natural treats are always a better choice, and often times cheaper.

The Water Bottle

Your guinea pigs water bottle is going to be their main source of water, and you're going to have to put fresh water in at least once a day. However, this might not be enough.

Guinea pigs are easily amused, and often enjoy playing games with their water bottle. There's nothing that you can do to stop these games, but be aware that you may have to clean up after them!

Note:

Guinea pigs love a routine, so you need to be sure to feed them at the same time (or times) every day, as this will give them comfort and security. You should vary minutes, not hours, with the exact time.

You should also remove the pellets after an hour or two of them being in there, or your guinea pig is going to nibble on them all day long. Because pellets are high in protein, they can cause your guinea pig to gain weight excessively.

Chapter Six:
Understanding Your Guinea Pig

That adorable little creature you have in your lap, hand, or cage isn't just a pet - he's an animal, and has some very specific and interesting characteristics that come with that.

For example, your guinea pig's wild counterparts are not only highly social animals, but they tend to live in herds - large herds at that, not just one or two of them.

For this reason, it's extremely important that your guinea pig always has a friend. Two guinea pigs housed together will create a special bond which will indeed last.

This chapter is set up a little differently then what you might be used to. We've broken it down into different sections, so you can flip to the specific problem that you're having - be it understanding what your guinea pig is trying to tell you, or if you want to lure your pet to eat from your hands.

To really understand your guinea pig, you need to spend time with them, learn their language, and connect with their feelings and thoughts. However, this chapter is your rough guide. Consider it the absolute basics of guinea pig 'speak', actions, and reactions.

Understanding Your Pets Need to Chew

You might roll your eyes when you see that your beloved pet has yet again chewed through that toilet paper roll, but don't get too annoyed. It's actually a very important thing!

Like most rodents, your guinea pig's teeth are going to continually grow throughout their entire life. Really, from the time of their birth, their teeth never stop growing.

Because of this, a guinea pig has a near undying need to chew. And boy, do they chew. The majority of their time is going to be spent chewing on something or another.

Make sure to regularly head to the local pet store and keep safe chew toys close at hand. Many owners also keep salt licks around, as they find it satisfies their pet when they're away.

If you want to go more organic, you *can* give your pet untreated branches and twigs from the tree out in the backyard. However, you *shouldn't* give your pet wood from cedar, apricot, peach or cherry trees, as this is extremely toxic to them.

The Pop-corning Effect

Have you ever noticed a guinea pig jumping straight up in the air, much like a piece of popcorn does when it's being cooked? Well, if you haven't, you're in for a treat.

This adorable and loveable reaction isn't out of the ordinary - he's doing it because he's simply too happy to contain himself. This is a wonderful sign that your guinea pig loves you, and is leading a happy life.

The Guinea Pig Behavior

As we've said, in the wild, guinea pigs form herds for safety and survival. These instincts are still a large part of the normal guinea pig attitude, and show in domesticated guinea pigs.

One of the biggest reasons that a guinea pig was domesticated for pets is because of their absolutely wonderful noises. When a guinea pig is completely content, he's going to coo like a baby, purr like a kitten, grunt like there's no tomorrow, and squeal with pleasure.

The Squealing

There is a fine line between a squeal of excitement and a squeal of fear, but with most guinea pigs you can tell the difference. When they suspect that food is in their near future, guinea pigs tend to squeal loudly.

This begging is actually exclusive to humans. In the wild, a guinea pig won't squeal excitedly... but then again, they have to actually roam to find their food!

If a guinea pig gets lonely, he's going to squeal loudly, searching for companionship and reassurance. While this is mostly seen in young guinea pigs, if a guinea pig is housed alone he will do the same thing.

If you hear a panicked squeal, suspect that your guinea pig is in danger. This is a natural reaction, and is used to warn others of the herd that something dangerous is coming their way.

The Cooing

These are huge signs of contentment, and you're going to often hear them as you're petting and loving them.

The Grumbling

If there's something that your guinea pig doesn't like, he's going to make a grumbling, rumbling sound that serves as a warning to those around him. You also can hear this when he hears a sound that he doesn't like.

The Nose Touch

Don't be startled if your guinea pig crawls right up your chest and touches his nose with yours. You should actually be honored as this shows that they like you quite a bit!

Feel free to do this with your guinea pig back, to show him that yes, you appreciate his affection - and you feel the same way that he does!

Here's an easy to read and handle chart to refer to if you're ever unsure what your pet means by the noises or actions that he's making.

Rises up with legs stiffened:
Threatening
Shows teeth with an open mouth:
Threatening
Stretches:
Comfort and relaxation
Popcorn jumping:
High spirits
Stretches head forward:
Watchfulness, interest
Grunts, gurgles, squeaks:
Contentment, and connection with other guinea pigs.
Squeals or shrieks:
Warning, loneliness, pain, fear
"Wheeting":
Begging for food
Cooing:
Reassurance
Rumbles:
Warning, dislike
Hisses, teeth clacking:
Aggression, threatening

The Intelligence of the Guinea Pig

When owning a guinea pig, you're going to hear people say, 'Oh, guinea pigs aren't smart! Why would you want a guinea *pig?*'. Don't listen to them at all, because they're completely wrong.

While you can't classify the guinea pig as a rocket scientist and he doesn't fall into the Albert Einstein range of brilliance; guinea pigs are alert, highly trainable, and respond very well.

Remember that the acts of hunting and scavenging isn't part of their natural programming, because they're herbivores. Their food is widely available, so they don't have to hunt.

In the wild the guinea pig has routes to and from its home that it's memorized so closely it can dart through them faster then a predator can follow.

When danger is suspected, the guinea pig herd has a most interesting mechanism for survival. They don't travel together as you can see herds of deer or zebra in the desert, but they utilize what's called a 'scatter response'.

This splits up the entire herd, and they all run in a different direction. This is to ensure that at least some of the herd survives. If they stay together, they run the risk of the entire herd being eaten.

Another interesting point to note is that in herds, when guinea pigs eat, there is always one who is a 'lookout' to watch for predators.

Taming

Your new, little guinea pig isn't going to always want to be held, and this can be an extreme disappointment to anyone hoping to just take their pig the first day they bring them home and cuddle.

However, what many owners find is that their pet is timid and rather shy. They tend to run away, squealing in fear of what they see as a giant hand coming to take them.

Slow movements and a quiet, calm voice are needed to coax your little guinea pigs out of hiding and into your loving arms. Remember to hold your young guinea pigs with a towel under them to avoid accidents (see, "When You Gotta Go, You Gotta Go", below).

You're going to want to coax your pet with treats to come out of hiding and into your hand. Develop trust slowly, and realize that it's going to take you a week or two to really forge a bond.

The First Few Days

The first 3-4 days you bring your guinea pig home, it can be very tempting to pick them up and cuddle with them. However, they're in a new area - and very scary area - and they need time to get used to that.

Give them several days to adjust to their new areas and life, because this is a very stressful time for them. Try to avoid making loud noises and hovering around them, because they need to take their own time to get used to what's around them.

Note:

You need to ensure that when you bring one or more guinea pigs into the house that they have a good area to hide. Each guinea pig needs his or her own place or a fight could break out!

Don't Loom!

Ever catch yourself just *looming* over your dear pet's cage, shadowing them as you're watching what they're doing? This is going to scare the sweet out of your little pet!

This makes your pet think that an eagle is swooping down to attack and causes him to be very scared. Instead, when you want to observe your pet, kneel down to eye level with the cage. This will allow him to see you as more of a friend, and less of a foe.

Bribery

The best way to get your pet to trust you is, without a doubt, bribery. Sound crazy? Perhaps. But it's true! Bribing the small animal that you want to love and adore is the best way for trust.

The best things to bribe with? *Treats*, of course. Because the guinea pig has so many things it loves to eat, you're going to have no shortage of bribing tools. Check out Chapter Five for more information on your guinea pig's favorite things to eat.

Start by showing your pet the delicious treat you're offering them, then set it at the open door of the cage. Sit just outside, with your hands in your lap, and wait.

After a certain amount of time, if he hasn't taken the treat, carefully and slowly pick it up again, close the cage door, and leave. Try this several times a day until he gets the idea that he has to come and get it.

Each time he comes, try to move a little closer to your pet's cage. This way, he's going to get used to your presence slowly.

After a while, he's going to be timid, but take the treat from your hand. If you give it enough time and patience, he's going to even welcome taking the treat from you, and won't be afraid to run and jump in excitement when he sees you coming.

To Pick Your Guinea Pig Up...

Don't lure your guinea pig with treats in order to pick him up, because you're going to hurt the tentative bond of trust you've built with him, and possibly damage any relationship in the future.

Instead, build trust by petting and loving your guinea pig, and showing him that you're not a scary predator, but instead a loving friend. Remember that in the wild, people like you would eat this poor little critter!

Be careful when you pick up your guinea pig! Because of the shape of their body, you can damage their lungs if you grasp them too hard.

Gently cup the torso of your guinea pig, and support the rear as you lift up. Don't hold them too hard, and instead carry them gently, ensuring that you're supporting their entire body well.

Remember to carry them with care, and small children should always hold their guinea pigs with great supervision - because of their small bone structure, they can be easily injured if dropped.

Relaxing Your Pet

Don't you just love the idea of sitting on your couch, petting your guinea pig in your lap, and reading the paper or watching the news? It's a great idea, but it takes a while.

When you first handle your guinea pig, do so in a quiet room, and make sure that nothing is going on. Have a treat ready, and see if you can get him to eat it on your lap.

If you're patient, he will, and eventually he's going to love being handled by you, and actually *request* it by squealing when he sees you coming near.

When You Gotta Go, You Gotta Go

Young guinea pigs should be handled with care, because they will simply go to the bathroom where ever they please. They simply don't know any better.

Because of this, you should always put a towel under a young guinea pig when you're holding him. This will prevent big accidents, and ensure that your guinea pig will never ruin your favorite pair of pants, or brand new white carpet.

As the guinea pig ages, he's going to start preferring to go in his own cage. This is his 'area', and sees it as a safer zone then in the wild.

When you have your guinea pig out, and he needs to *go*, you're going to be able to tell. He'll act extremely nervous by prancing around, and tend to back up into corners.

When this happens, simply lift your guinea pig and place him in his cage. After you've given him a few minutes of privacy to do his deed, feel free to take him out again for more playing.

Regular Schedules

It's important, especially in the first few months, that you try and stick to the same, regular schedule of feeding your guinea pigs. At the same time every day ensure that they get fed.

Soon, your guinea pig will squeal in delight when he hears the rustle of a food bag or the opening of the refrigerator. This is a good way to create a bond, and give your guinea pig the sense of a regular schedule.

Exercise and Movement

Just as it's essential for we as humans to have plenty of exercise, guinea pigs need exercise to stay fit and healthy. Without it, guinea pigs are at a higher risk for heart conditions and more.

There are actually many different ways that your guinea pig can get the exercise they need to feel good and healthy. The best way is to set up an area on a clean floor (avoid carpet).

You can block off a decent size area in a corner, and let them out to run and enjoy themselves. Each guinea pig should have a hiding place, and plenty of room to run around.

Bringing toys - like a toilet paper roll stuffed with hay - can be a wonderful treat for your little piggy. What's better is hiding their favorite foods in different areas, and see how long it takes them to discover what's hidden.

PVC pipes around the area is also a source of unending entertainment for guinea pigs, who adore to race through them and find new 'tracks' to have fun with.

Simple things like paper bags are always a treat as well. A small, untreated cardboard box with a guinea -pig size hole will leave them feeling secure and having fun.

Don't be afraid to keep them in their area for an hour or more at a time, because your guinea pig is going to enjoy being out of his cage. Soon, he's going to look forward to his taste of freedom each day.

A bigger cage also gives your guinea pig a chance to run off some excess energy - and never have to leave his home. A 'two story' cage can help your guinea pig keep up his agility, and gives him more room in less actual space.

When you're designing their cage, and figuring out exactly where to put your pigs things, remember to place things around to encourage movement - food, shelter, water... it should all come together so that your guinea pig gets the most exercise in the space he can get.

Remember to always remove the items that have been soiled or chewed on too much - a paper bag isn't fun when it's wet with guinea pig urine, after all.

Note:

Many people have exercise wheels or balls that they can place their guinea pig in so that they can run around. They see this as a valid exercise tool, and therefore they don't need to take them out.

You shouldn't use these, however, as they can seriously injure your pet. The spine, legs, and feet can all be hurt in these balls, so try to avoid them as much as possible.

Chapter Seven:
Grooming Your Guinea Pig

Despite what some people say, guinea pigs are extremely low maintenance pets and easy to take care of. However, they do require some day-to-day care.

The Nails

Your guinea pig's nails are going to need trimming or they will get long and painful.

Giving your guinea pigs rocks, rough stones, bricks, and other, similar surfaces can really help wear down their nails. Bricks are the cheapest and best solution, but make sure that they don't have holes in them!

Like other animals guinea pigs have blood vessels in their nails. This is commonly referred to as the quick. In nails that are clear in color, it's easy to see them - basically the pink area that extends from the bone to the toe. However, in black nails, the quick is nearly impossible to spot.

With clear nails, all you need to do is cut just past the pinkish area.

With black nails, many owners choose to cut their guinea pigs nails very little and more often. It's not impossible to cut a longer black nail without cutting the quick, though it does take time and practice.

If you end up cutting the quick, you will need to stop the bleeding. Many pet stores sell 'Quick Stop', which will stop the bleeding altogether. If you don't have this, put iodine on the nail instead.

Your guinea pig is likely to squirm a lot during this process. If you've got help to cut the nail, this is going to be easier to do. Wrap your guinea pig in a towel and make sure the feet are sticking out. Have one person hold the guinea pig while the other cuts the nails.

If you're going solo, place your guinea pig on a tennis racket so that their nails are sticking out, and cover them so that they feel more secure.

The Teeth

Like most rodents, your Guinea pig has two incisors that are constantly growing. If they grow too long, you need to take your guinea pig to the vet to get them cut or your pig won't be able to eat.

Eating hard foods keeps these teeth in check, which is why you should always keep things in the cage for your pet to chew on - like toilet paper rolls, for instance.

Many people give their guinea pigs hay cubes or old, stale bread to help them keep their teeth shorter as well, but this doesn't mean you don't have to inspect them regularly.

Check their teeth and make sure that nothing is chipped or broken, because this is bad for your guinea pig. If something has broken or fallen out, you need to contact your vet.

Brushing

You should regularly brush your guinea pig to keep their coat clean, shining, and healthy. For long-haired guinea pigs, daily brushing is vital. For short- haired guinea pigs, a few times a week works well.

Use a soft baby's brush with gentle bristles, as this will make your guinea pig truly enjoy it. For longer fur that might get tangled, try a metal greyhound comb. This will remove all of the excess hair and lessen shedding.

Bathing

Let's get one thing clear. Guinea pigs don't like to be bathed. They become highly stressed when you do decide to dunk them in water, and this can lower their immune system.

Many guinea pigs go their entire lives without bathing, and that's just fine for them. Unless you've been instructed by the vet, or your guinea pig got into something dirty and smelly, you do not have to bathe him.

If you do have to bathe him, choose a shampoo that's light on his skin - either something made for kittens (not cats) or a baby shampoo. Only use a medicated shampoo if it's recommended by a vet.

Chapter Eight:
Guinea Pig Diseases
& Common Health Problems

Our guinea pigs are wonderful creatures, and extremely loving, but they're also extremely fragile, and are more prone to illness then other pets which can mean vet visits in your future.

Guinea pigs can both have sudden illnesses, and gradual symptoms that add up to something bigger. The only thing that you can do is really pay attention to your guinea pig, and know when something is wrong.

Make sure to always watch how much they consume, both in food and water, and try to regularly gauge their activity as a guinea pig who isn't active is often sick.

We've listed some of the most common symptoms your guinea pig can experience, and what they usually mean. If you're worried about your piggy, just hop to one of these and figure out what's wrong, and if it's serious.

If in doubt, call the vet! They'll be able to tell you for sure, so if you can't see it here, you need to get it checked out.

Sneezing, Discharge of the Nose

Guinea pigs often sneeze - it's completely normal, and you'd sneeze, too, if you were hanging out with hay the entire day! Excessive sneezing is often because of a respiratory issue, though.

Sometimes, your guinea pig can become allergic to his bedding - especially if it's a soft wood, or especially dusty hay. Try to change the bedding and see if that makes a difference, or remove him from the area completely.

If your pet has any sort of discharge around the nose, you need to get it checked out. The same goes if you see your guinea pig rubbing his nose, because this is often because of a discharge.

Guinea pigs actually don't catch *colds*, at least not the way we do. Their respiratory issues are the cause of bacteria, not a virus.

Coughing

Like in most humans, some coughing is completely normal. Caused by an irritation in the throat, it's mostly because of inhaling dusty hay or something else small.

Constant coughing can be serious, and usually is with an infection, or some sort of illness. If your guinea pig is coughing and is accompanied by wheezing, or labored breathing, you need to contact your vet as it is most likely a respiratory infection of some sort.

Labored Breathing, or Wheezing of Any Sort

Take this symptom very seriously. This is often a sign of a respiratory infection, and needs to be treated sooner rather than later. It's usually because of congestion in the lungs and can easily become pneumonia if left untreated.

Scratching

Some scratching, again, is normal - it's just part of their body! Excessive scratching is normally a sign of parasites, most likely lice or mites. A fungal infection will also cause scratching.

You can tell if your pet has a parasite by brushing through their hair and looking at the skin. Lice will be shown clearly on the skin and are normally a small brown color.

If your pet has lice, you can get a medicated shampoo from your doctor that will kill the lice without hurting your guinea pig. Most of the time, you're going to have to shampoo him twice - once, and then again a week to two weeks from the first wash.

This ensures that you get not only the lice, but the lice that hatch from the current eggs. Lice can be very tricky to get rid of, but a medicated shampoo usually does the trick.

Mites are much harder to kill and spot and actually can't be seen with the naked eye. There are some home remedies out there to help with mites, but the best option is to get care from your vet.

With parasites, you should always clean and disinfect the cage.

Milky-White Urine or Sludge-y Bladder

Normally, the urine a guinea pig produces has a slightly milky color to it, and this is completely normal. However, if your guinea pig has extremely clear/white urine, or his urine is overly sludge-y, this could mean that he has a higher-then-normal calcium level in his diet.

Removing any foods that might be high in calcium can often times correct this, but this can lead to bladder stones in some guinea pigs. Call the vet to be sure.

Pink or Red Urine

This is serious, as it means that there is blood in your guinea pig's urine. It's often an indicator of uroliths, which is simply bladder stones. These are also very serious.

If your guinea pig has blood in his urine, you should get to him to the vet as soon as possible. To help prevent bladder stones, a diet high in water and even cranberry juice. This can help break down already formed or forming stones and really help your guinea pig.

Diarrhea or Extremely Soft Stool

Don't take this lightly! Within hours of suffering from diarrhea, your guinea pig can die if it persists. The dehydration they experience isn't just serious, but deadly.

Often times, you've simply fed your pet too many wet foods or vegetables in general. For a few days go easy on the treats and see if the that helps your pet.

Another good option if you think its food related is to increase your pets intake of hay, which promotes a good digestive balance.

No matter what the reason for the diarrhea, there *is* something you can do to help your pet, and it's important that you try to take care of it as soon as you notice that.

Head to a health food store or a pharmacy and grab some lactobacillus acidophilus in capsule form. You don't need a prescription, it's available over the counter.

Taking half a capsule and dissolve it in 1 cc of water. Taking a syringe (without the needle, of course!), fill it with the water and place the top into his mouth. Slowly squeeze the syringe so that he can drink the water.

Make sure that he drinks it slowly, so that he doesn't choke!

The medicine promotes good bacterial growth in the stomach that can help digestion of normal foods, and will generally make your guinea pig feel better.

Some people suggest feeding your guinea pig yogurt, which does the same thing. But yogurt a dairy product - bad for your pet, and you have to feed them more of it for the same results.

Antibiotics kill good and bad bacteria, so if your guinea pig is put on antibiotics, you should really give them a supplement of acidophilus as a preventive measure.

Hair Loss

There are many different reasons for hair loss in a guinea pig, including mites that burrow under the skin and create sores, which cause the hair loss.

If your guinea pig is cut or bitten, the hair will fall out in that area until the skin is completely healed. This is nothing to worry about, and is completely normal.

Massive hair loss across the body is caused by ringworm, and sometimes ovarian cysts. Unless it's because of a cut, you should call your vet and see how he would like to proceed.

Watery Eyes

Watery eyes are often caused by irritants in the eye, like excessive dust or something more. Allergies can also cause this. Call your vet and ask for directions on how to rinse the irritants out of the eye.

Sometimes eye sores are caused by cysts on the eyelid that irritate the eyes, and these need to be removed by a trained veterinarian as they can be painful and serious.

Stiff Joints

See your piggy having a hard time walking? Sometimes it happens - most times, it's caused by scurvy. Yes, your guinea pig can actually get scurvy

This is basically a severe lack of vitamin C, and needs to be treated immediately. Call your vet to schedule an appointment. Most likely, he'll inject your guinea pig with vitamin C to correct the deficiency.

Make sure that your pig is getting at least 10 mg a day!

Tilting Head

If your piggy is tilting his head to one side and having issues walking, it's probably a middle ear infection that's throwing off his balance and hurting his ear and head.

Get him to the vet as soon as you possibly can because this can damage his hearing and more.   Basically, you need to get it treated and not put it off.

Seizures

Watching your guinea pig have a seizure is an extremely scary thing, so calm down for a moment and think clearly.

There are two 'types' of seizures, so pay attention to what he's doing. If his head is straight up in the air, without a tilt at all, then he's probably got mites. Mites burrow under the skin and can sometimes affect the nervous system. Get him to a vet for treatment, and he'll be just fine.

If your guinea pig is tilting his head to one side or curling his body during the seizure, it can be a huge number of any things, including a genetic disorder or dietary issues.

Head to the vet as soon as possible, and get blood tests done. He'll be able to pinpoint the exact reason that your guinea pig is having seizures. The frequency and severity of the seizures will also help determine if they need to be treated, and how.

The majority of seizures involve a head lift or tilt, and twitching of both the muscles and the eyes. The twitching of the eyes can last several minutes after the muscle twitching has gone away.

Don't be frightened if your guinea pig squeals, screeches, or grunts during a seizure - that often happens.

Eating Feces

In some animals, this would indicate that something is wrong; however, in guinea pigs it's actually completely normal. It's from when they were in the wild, actually.

The guinea pig feces is full of vitamins that they were not able to process the first time around, and their body has no problem digesting it again. There's nothing wrong with this, so don't worry.

Finding a Vet

There is *no* question at all - you should provide regular vet checkups to your guinea pig, and it's essential that you find a good quality vet before you experience an emergency.

You can't go to a 'regular' vet for your guinea pig. You actually need a special vet for exotic animals, which can be hard to find. Make sure to ask plenty of question before you choose your vet, including:

-       Have you treated guinea pigs before?
-       What antibiotic (s) do you prefer to prescribe to adult guinea pigs with an upper respiratory infection? (Bayril, Chloramphenicol, and Doxycycline are all great choices. As you're going to read below, avoid anything based in penicillin!)
-       Are you an 'exotic animal veterinarian'?
-       What are your hours?

-       Can Baytril be used on young
        puppies? (of course, this is a big no)
-       What are you policies about
        emergencies?
-       What sorts of foods do you
        recommend feeding a guinea pig on a
        daily basis? (avoid the answer
        'alfalfa'! Look for Timothy hay or
        good quality pellets)

And anything else that is important to you.

Make sure that your needs, and your guinea
pigs needs, are met by your vet. If they're
not, do not feel guilty about switching.
There are just some things that need to be
met.

The best way to pick a vet is by word of
mouth, so if you know any friends with
guinea pigs, ask them if they like a certain
vet, and why. You can also call regular vets
and ask them who they recommend as an
exotic animal vet, and see if one name
sticks out.

Note:

Drugs that include penicillin are extremely
toxic to guinea pigs, so ask your vet each
time a new drug is prescribed if it's

penicillin-based or not. Do not just blindly trust your vet!

Also, Baytril (a wonderful antibiotic for guinea pigs) is dangerous for puppies, so keep this in mind!

My Guinea Pig is Sick - Help!

The first thing to do if you discover that your guinea pig is sick is to separate him from any other guinea pigs that are in the cage, as you don't know if what he has is infectious.

Call the vet, and calmly explain exactly what's wrong. If it's serious, they're going to schedule you in as soon as possible.

Oh No! It's The Weekend/Evening! What Do I Do?!

So, it's the weekend and your guinea pig needs to be seen by a vet – soon.   Head to your phone book and look for an emergency hours vet. While you might be charged a little more, you're able to get the treatment your guinea pig needs sooner rather then later.

Can't find anything in the phone book?
Head online, and search for a vet in your
area that will take animals at all hours.

Often times, vets will have other people
working - a veterinary assistant, for
example - that will be able to help your pet
and get them the treatment that they need.

It's Scary

The little animal that you love and care for
is sick, and it's a scary thought. But don't
panic, and make sure that you stay calm.
The worst thing you can do is upset your
guinea pig more, and put stress of them as
well.

Remember that guinea pigs are very good
at hiding their issues as they are animals of
prey. Pay attention, and if something seems
off like lack of energy or loss of appetite.

Chapter Nine:
Breeding Guinea Pigs

Puppies (baby guinea pigs) are possibly the cutest little things that you can find, according to many owners of guinea pigs, and they absolutely adore the little ones.

However, you should think carefully before you really take the leap to breed your guinea pigs and raise puppies for nurturing. Not only is it extremely time consuming, but without even meaning to you can expand your little guinea 'herd' to dozens.

Most people choose not to breed simply because they don't have the room for the extra piggies. Others realize that they don't have the time, or money, to keep the little puppies.

If you do decide to breed and eventually sell your guinea pigs, do your research first. Some areas are already overflowing with guinea pig breeders, and you could be contributing to an overpopulation of guinea pigs in a certain area.

If you're dead-set on breeding your piggies, here are some things to remember and purchase before you even consider it!

-    You're going to need room for the puppies as they grow older, and after they get so old, you're going to want to separate the females from the males. That means you're going to need at least another cage, if not two, with enough room for three-five guinea pigs at a time.

-    You will need enough guinea pig bedding, food, and hay to feed all of these little mouths until you sell the guinea pigs.

-    The attention that you give your puppies are very important, and they should be handled from a very young age. Why, you ask? Well, the more they're handled when they're young, the easier they will be to train as they age!

-    Vet fee's! You never know what's going to happen, and an emergency vet visit could be in your future. You

need to make sure you have enough
to cover any surprise visits.

- You need to be sure that you have
  enough knowledge to speak clearly
  about guinea pigs with the potential
  buyers, and explain exactly what
  they need to do with their guinea
  pigs. You also should have a list to
  give them on basic care for guinea
  pigs.

- Hundreds, if not thousands, of guinea
  pigs die each year because their
  owners are unable to take care of
  them, or let them breed excessively.
  It's good to have a family or families
  in mind that will want your puppies
  before you breed your guinea pigs,
  because then you know they're going
  to a good home.

Still convinced that you want to breed your
guinea pigs? Get ready because this is not
just a let-nature-take-it's-course kind of
birth!

The Mating

So, you want to mate your guinea pigs.
That's fine, but you're going to need a
male and a female guinea pig, and neither

of them should be spayed or nurtured (you can see the issue with this, I'm sure).

The female should be four to six months old when she first gives birth.

As nature intended, you're going to want to give your guinea pigs plenty of space. The female cycle is about 16 days, but the female will only be able to mate between 8-24 hours of that.

When the male is aroused, he's going to lower his head and walk towards the female. His steps won't be random. This is a deliberate act to entice his love interest.

The rumbling sound they make is very distinct, so don't be nervous if you've never heard it before. His bottom will even wag side-to-side several times.

The males can sometimes even do a mating 'dance', where they will put their front legs on anything that's available and move to attract his female. This can include side to side waving, wiggling, and waggling.

While this is very humorous to watch, remember that this mating ritual has been intact for hundreds of years, and it has evolved to be the best the species can bring. That being said, it's polite to leave the room if you're going to laugh!

If the female is interested, she's going to start squeaking with anxiety and excitement, and these squeaks are going to be louder the closer the male guinea pig is to her.

If she isn't interested - either she's not in heat, or just not the right time during her cycle - she's going to snap and bite him, and even run away. If the male is extremely persistent, she may urinate on his face to get the message through.

If a female is ready when the male isn't aroused, she may walk towards him with the same deliberate steps that he used on her, head down and rear end up in the air slightly.

Sometimes, a woman will even back into the male as a sign that she wants him to mount her. This isn't at all unusual, so don't be frightened if you see something you're just not sure about. They know what they're doing.

The Pregnancy

When your female guinea pig is pregnant, she's going to about double her weight - which means that she's going to eat a bit more then she usually does, so you need to take that into account.

She is also going to be drinking more water then usual, so you might have to refill her water bottle more then usual. Don't worry - this is all natural, and because she needs to gain sufficient weight to take care of her puppies.

She's also going to be needing more vitamin C than she used to - about twice the normal amount, or at least 20 mgs a day. You should ensure that her treats are filled with it - parsley, cabbage, and dandelion greens are all great options for this budding mother.

She's going to have a gestation period of between 60 and 70 days, and the longer the gestation, the smaller the litter. If your guinea pig has a shorter gestation period, her litter is going to be larger.

While it's not necessary to remove the guinea pig while she's pregnant, you should within the last week of birth, mostly because within hours of giving birth, mama guinea pig is going to be ready to mate again, which isn't healthy at all.

As your guinea pig mother (commonly referred to as a sow) reaches the second month of her pregnancy, she's going to be become visibly plump.

You're going to be able to feel the puppies inside her stomach, and sometimes even estimate how many puppies she's going to have. As the babies start moving and kicking inside of her, she is about three weeks away from giving birth.

And finally, while your guinea pig is pregnant you need to avoid any radical changes in her lifestyle. Stress on a pregnant guinea pig can be fatal for the puppies in her.

The Birth of the Guinea Piglets

Luckily for you, there's nothing that you have to do during the actual birth of the puppies. They will most likely be born between dawn and dusk, which is when the guinea pigs are at their peak of activity.

There's really no way of knowing when your guinea pig is going to into labor, but if you're able to be present for the birth, it's best to watch quietly from afar.

The puppies will usually be born about five minutes apart, and the entire birthing sequence should take no longer then a half an hour. If it does, take your guinea pig to the vet as soon as possible.

With each contraction that she has, she's going to push out the babies. As they come out, she will reach down and break the sack that covers each puppy.

After each puppy is born, she was pass what is called the placenta. This will then be eaten by her - it's all normal, and means that there is very little mess left over.

The mother will finally lick the babies clean, and the father can sometimes assist in this duty, if he's around. Remember that he needs to be removed, though as he will impregnate the female soon after, and this is extremely stressful on the guinea pig.

After the mother has done her duties, she's going to lead them to a corner of the cage. They will huddle under her for warmth and milk.

Caring for the Little Ones

A young guinea pig is nearly completely independent from his mother. They only require the warmth and milk from their mum. They're born with teeth, claws, hair, and completely open eyes.

In fact, they're going to be running around the cage within *hours* of being born, and they will start eating solid food within a day. It's a surprising difference when you look at kittens, who are helpless not just for days, but weeks.

The mother guinea pig only has two teats, but there is rarely fighting over who will drink from mum first. Because they can eat independently, they're more then willing to wait their turn.

This is the most important time in a young guinea pigs life to form serious and lasting connections with a human. Unlike some mammals, a mother guinea pig *will not* reject her babies if they've been handled by a human.

That means you're free to touch, pet, and hold these babies as much as humanly possible. The more you care for them directly, the more comfortable they're going to be with people in general.

Weaning

The guinea pigs are going to naturally wean themselves off of their mother's milk within the third week. By four weeks old, the guinea pigs are going to need to be separated as the males can actually impregnate their own mother.

By four weeks, you should be able to give your guinea pigs away or sell them, as you wish. While a guinea pig will be very frightened away from the only home he's known, they will feel better after adjusting.

Complications During Birth

Not all pregnancies can go smoothly, and there are sometimes complications that can develop. You should have on hand the number of your vet to ensure that if something happens you can take your guinea pig in.

While it's not a complication, a common mishap is that your guinea pig won't break the sack that contains the baby in time.

Some people mistake this for stillbirth - it's not, however.

If you're witnessing the birth and see the guinea pig ignoring her just-birthed baby, take the puppy and break the membrane that is over their nose and mouth.

Open the small mouth, and gently blow several small breaths in rapid succession down the babies throats - as best you can, of course. To increase circulation and stimulate a heart beat, move his legs around gently.

If the baby gasps or makes a noise, you may be able to save him. Keep him warm in your hands and gently blow down his throat until you can find a cloth to dry his body. Rub him gently with the cloth.

Once the guinea pig starts to squeak, you're well on your way.

Keep the puppy warm, but don't give him anything to eat or drink at all. Ensure that he's wrapped in a towel, and near a heat source - like a warm water bottle.

This will keep the baby from catching the chills, which can make him sick.

After about an hour - until the baby can stand on his own - you can try and introduce him to his mother. She's not going to actually recognize the baby as hers, so just gently put it under her body and watch.

If she does reject the child, you can try again, but chances are, she's not going to accept the baby guinea pig.

Hand Raising Guinea Pigs

For one reason or another, guinea pig mothers may very well reject their children. Sometimes there is no reason - but it does happen.

When that happens, chances are you're going to have to hand-rear the babies yourself. This can get complicated, but it is completely possible.

The first option you should explore, however, is adding your new little one to another litter. If you have a guinea pig mother that has recently given birth, this is the best option.

What you should do is remove the mother's litter, and rub the new baby against the other puppies. This way, the orphaned guinea pig will pick up their scent.

Slowly introduce the guinea pig babies back, and watch closely. If the mother accepts the baby as her own, then you have nothing to worry about. But this isn't going to always happen.

If the mother rejects the guinea pig, you're going to know very quickly, and remember to remove the puppy she's rejected right away.

Raising a guinea pig by yourself is time consuming, but can be very rewarding. Every two hours, starting when you wake up in the morning, you need to feed your guinea pig baby a milk substitute.

Contact your vet and ask what's the best for the guinea pig. Sometimes they will carry a special formula specifically for guinea pig puppies who have been rejected by their mothers.

Feeding tips, along with more detailed instructions, can all be found at a vet's office. Often times, pet stores will carry feeding tools for kittens that work well.

After each feeding, wash their mouths gently to get rid of any spilled milk, because it can spoil on the coat and make it sticky. You're going to need to do this for the first four days.

If you're housing the baby guinea pig(s) with the father, you may see him licking the anus and genital organs if they're not together. If he isn't doing that, you're going to need to wipe that area with a clean, damp cloth to stimulate urination and bowel movements. Pay close attention, because this needs to be done!

After the fourth day, your guinea pig is ready and willing to eat hard food. If the father guinea pig is housed in the same cage, chances are they will already have learned.

If not, place a young guinea pig in the cage with the babies, and they will be able to pick up the idea of eating solid food very quickly. guinea pigs are extremely observant creatures, after all.

Lack of Milk

Sometimes, a young mother won't have enough milk to sufficiently feed her entire brood. It's very unfortunate when this happens, but it isn't unusual when a mother guinea pig is simply too young.

You have two options in this situation. You can relocate a few babies to another mother who has had her children under ten days ago, or you can provide a milk substitute to help compliment the mother's milk.

Chapter 10:
The Elder Guinea Pig

During a guinea pig's life span, they become wonderful friends, amazing companions, and they can really become a part of your family. Sharing a bond with this sort of animal is hard to compare with anything else so wonderful.

Guinea pig aging and death can be very hard, especially for children who feel a bond with their animal stronger then adults. But it happens, and you should be prepared.

The Life Span & Aging

Guinea pigs can live anywhere between 5-10 years, depending on the breed and the level of care that they have. Even the size of the cage and the amount of exercise they get can have an impact on their life span.

Female guinea pigs tend to lead shorter lives then their male counterparts, but

some guinea pigs will surprise you. One
guinea pig who was famous online lived for
over 11 years, quite a run for a healthy pig.

Guinea pig aging is very similar to ours.
They exercise less, eat less, drink less,
sleep more, move slower, and get less
excited then they used to about simple
things.

They can also experience a number of
issues that are simply related with old age,
including arthritis. This is all common of
your guinea pig leading a long, happy life.

Many vets will reluctantly treat a guinea pig
who is older, because stressing them
excessively can bring them an early grave.
It's just as important to have a reliable
routine for your guinea pigs in their old age
as it was in their young years.

When a Guinea Pig's Spouse Dies

Guinea pigs form strong bonds with each
other when they're in the same cage.
When one dies, it can be very traumatizing
to the other guinea pigs in the cage. If
there's only two and one dies, the second
guinea pig is going to get extremely lonely.

Introducing a new guinea pig is always a decent idea, but give your guinea pig time to grieve the loss.   Bringing him new toys or goodies can also improve his mood, and help him get past the loss.

As your guinea pig ages, remember to avoid stressing him as much as possible. Give them plenty of goodies and enough cuddles that he's going to be content, and fight a little longer to stay in your arms.

If your guinea pig is suffering from hair loss, labored breathing, or complete loss of an appetite, call your veterinarian and see if there is anything they can do.

Sometimes a guinea pig is just too old, but there are some things that you can do to ensure that they're comfortable and content in their last weeks, months, or even days.

Death Isn't Pretty

There's nothing nice about the death of someone you care about, so give yourself time to grieve, too. It's not 'just a guinea pig', but you've lost a wonderful companion who really cared about you, and trusted you fully.

Explaining to children where a guinea pig has gone can be extremely hard, but often times, the truth is the best option. This is hard for everyone, so respect that they're having trouble understanding just what happened with the pet they've loved and cared about for so long.

23443556R00066

Made in the USA
Lexington, KY
13 June 2013